A New Gym for At-Risk Youth
A Not-for-Profit Starter's Guide

How to Create a Fitness/Mentoring Not-For-Profit Organization for At-Risk Youth

By Willem C. Kiefer

Dedication-

This brief text is dedicated to all of the members of the Bench Mark Program community who travelled the journey alongside me as I collected the experiences that now constitute this text. I am especially grateful to my wife Karla, who had to deal with my near insanity "behind closed doors" when I was burdened with the lack of direction that is so common in starting a business. I hope this text will be a tool for you to find some direction and persevere in your own similar endeavors.

Preface-

This text was originally compiled as a deliverable component to a business-development consulting contract. After the contract was completed I recognized that perhaps others might benefit from a brief guide to launching a mentoring program based on fitness and recreation. The content herein is designated specifically for those who are looking to start a program in this unique sector of the non-profit world. I do not claim to be an expert in "all things start-up," but I do feel somewhat qualified to offer advice on something that I have actually done in my own professional career.

This is the guide that I wish I had discovered when I started my non-profit start-up journey in my final year of college. My hope is that I can save you time and energy searching for direction so that you can focus more on putting your team in place to create a solution to the problem that you have identified. If you are passionate about bringing together the fields of fitness, mentoring, and leadership, then this guide can help you move through the details of start-up.

This guide also specifically references a program created to serve the at-risk youth population, and many of the connections listed are connections that would be critical for a program serving the same population. If you are hoping to serve another sector of the population completely distinct from the at-risk youth population, I cannot promise that this first version of the guide (as written) will be of great service to you.

My ultimate hope is that this guide will increase the number of individuals who see the possibility of starting up their own businesses to serve at-risk youth across our nation. In order to effectively serve all of the at-risk youth in need in distinct neighborhoods across the nation, we will need a proportionate number of distinct resources to fit their interests. What follows is my contribution to the puzzle of finding effective programming for at-risk youth in need of support.

-Willem C. Kiefer

Table of Contents:

Chapter 1: About Bench Mark Program..6
Chapter 2: Start Up Checklist 8
Chapter 3: Key Player Checklist 10
Chapter 4: Legal/Financial Compliance Checklist 12
Chapter 5: Connection Web | Generating Referrals 13
Chapter 6: Conversation Break-down Sheet | School District and Guidance Counselors14
Chapter 7: Conversation Break-down Sheet | Juvenile Probation....................................16
Chapter 8: Conversation Break-Down Sheet | Clinical Therapy Offices...........................18
Chapter 9: Conversation Break-Down Sheet | Other Programs and Detention Centers .20
Chapter 10: Conversation Break-Down Sheet | Donors 21
Chapter 11: Staffing/Volunteer Guidelines 23
Chapter 12: Grant Writing Checklist 25
Chapter 13: Model Description 27

Chapter 1
About Bench Mark Program

While I was a student at Franklin and Marshall College (Lancaster, PA Class of 2014) I couldn't shake the feeling that I needed to do something "more" with my time and energy. I was wrapping up my senior year while I searched for some way to give back to the Lancaster City community. Without any particular skills or certifications to mentor/coach anyone, I thought I might be able to have an impact on some teenagers with low self-esteem. I reasoned that If I could simply get a small group of them to exercise with me on a regular basis, I could easily help build self-confidence through exercise and self-confidence, and in turn, help propel teenagers toward healthy life decisions.

As with all good ideas, my plan became infinitely more complicated when I actually began to work with my original three students. I was connected with three male teenagers from a local high school through a professor at F&M College who knew a director at the Spanish American Civic Association. After picking the three young men up from school almost every day and taking them to workout at the local YMCA, we quickly became friends. Conversation flowed naturally in between our exercise sets and I became aware of some serious challenges in their lives. Coming from a middle-class (comfortable) background, these were challenges that I had never dealt with, but I reasoned that I could probably help out a bit with the "simple stuff." Simple stuff refers to: helping with homework, writing resumes, talking through tough friend situations, talking about college, driving to job interviews, and filling out the FAFSA (stuff parents might normally do) just to name a few items. All the while I was operating off the belief (somehow this became lodged in my brain/heart) that "to whom much is given, much is owed" and I felt good helping out as I could between college coursework.

By the time that I graduated from F&M in May, 2014 (only 4 months after my original group began) I had 15-20 high school students attending our nightly gym sessions for free personal training and what we began to call "mentoring." News of our operation was spreading through word of mouth. Interestingly, I came to learn that most of my students were involved with the local Office of Juvenile Probation, the Children and Youth Agency, or one of handful of local clinical therapy offices. Our eclectic "gym family" was starting to take shape, and I knew that I couldn't leave Lancaster and abandon this group of young people who had come to lean on me for advice/support.

In the span of 3 months I graduated, picked up a part-time job to support myself, decided to formalize the program by filing for non-profit status with the IRS, and started to look for gym space outside of the YMCA. I had gathered a group of adults to serve as fellow mentors to the group of at-risk youth, and together we had decided that this budding program was valuable in the community. I was starting to see the beginning of some semblance of proof of concept.

What followed from mid-2014 to early 2017 can be related to a football player putting her head down and running through a tunnel of other, much larger players, trying to knock her down, often times dealing seriously discouraging blows. The details of this "hustle" do not belong in this brief text, but I will simply say that with an incredibly small budget, our program had to prove (over the course of multiple years) that our services were valuable. Without basing our service off of a cookie-cutter, evidence based strategy for mentoring, we had to prove that our homemade strategy for mentoring was effective. Unfortunately, during this time we neglected to collect appropriate data on our own mentoring strategy (which we are doing now, actually), so I hope to caution you in the following text to focus heavily on data collection in your own start-up period. But I digress. Even without the hard evidence (on paper) that our services were useful, our "little free gym" had helped enough young people turn their lives around that we were able to establish strategic partnerships anyway. And therein lies the key to sustainability: strategic partnership and steady contract funding (at least in our case).

By the start of 2017, our little "gym family" has become a "big gym family." We have two gym facilities and a healthy stream of referrals from the Office of Juvenile Probation, Children and Youth Agency, 3 local school districts, and 4 local clinical therapy offices. We have a team of dedicated mentors and a growing executive staff, and we are being to clean up our operating policy and procedure to make our board's governance committee and insurance agent happy. Most importantly, we have created a space where older at-risk youth (who sometimes feel like they don't belong in other programs) can come for hope and inspiration. Bench Mark Program has expanded beyond my wildest dreams, and it is beginning to change the way we look at mentoring, and connecting with at-risk youth who are constantly portrayed as destructive and criminally minded by the local media. A new definition of "community gym" is starting to form, and Bench Mark Program is leading the charge. Our facilities now have a distinct feel, a certain atmosphere that can be felt after walking in and hanging out for a few minutes. That feeling is captivating to most of us who rarely have been surrounded by so much positivity and encouragement.

And yet we still have a LONG way to go, and much to learn. I chose to write about our adventures and experiences thus far so that you can accelerate your concept to the point where Bench Mark Program currently sits: out of the start-up phase and into the sustainable growth phase. The later stage will no doubt be the topic of a second book, but I hope that the following text can give you some clarity on effective strategies to thrive in the first phase: start-up.

Chapter 2
Start-up Checklist

The following is a list of essential components to the start up of your not-for-profit organization (hereafter referred to as "ABC"). The list is set up in chronological order (1-first, 10-last) so that by completing each task, you are one step closer to the operation of a sustainable corporation. The start-up phase, for these purposes, encompasses the first 6 months of operation.

1.) Proof of Concept

a.) Is the service that ABC intends to provide "in demand?" Can you support this claim with statistics relevant to the area where your corporation will operate? Do you have anecdotal evidence from a trial run? Do you have proof of support (both financial and non-financial) from community members and businesses? Have you identified model programs that serve as points of comparison to your corporation?

2.) Business Incorporation and IRS Not-for-Profit Designation

a.) It is recommended that in order to expedite this process, you consult with an attorney or other legal professional. Otherwise, there are online resources that allow you complete these steps on your own (with risk of error).

b.) Is your business legally incorporated in the state in which you intend to operate?

c.) Does the IRS recognize your corporation as not-for-profit with a unique EIN number?

3.) Establish a Board of Directors and Bylaws

a.) In order to become incorporated as an official not-for-profit organization, you will need to establish a Board of Directors (* See "Key Player Checklist" for more information) and a set of Bylaws that will govern the Board of Directors.

4.) Identify and ratify a policy and procedure manual.

a.) It is crucial to open your operation with a set of rules that you, your staff, and you clients can all abide by. Specifically, to avoid tragic emergency situations, you need to have a document to reference when something unexpected occurs.

b.) There are generic policy and produce manuals available for your review and amendment online.

5.) Initial Round of Start-up Fundraising

a.) (*See Donor Conversation Sheet for more details)

b.) Leverage your Board of Directors and community supporters to raise money for the following start-up costs over 6 months (*costs vary depending on location):

i.) Incorporation/Legal Fees (approximately $2000)

ii.) Insurance Coverage (approximately $4000)

iii.) Facility Rental/Lease (approximately $4-$5/sqft/year or $8000)

    iv.)   Equipment (minimal) (approximately $5000)
    v.)   Staff Stipend (approximately $6000)
    vi.)   **Total: $25,000**

6.)   Acquire liability insurance for your organization's facility, your staff, and your executive leadership.

    a.)   It is recommended that you "shop around" with multiple professional insurance brokers to determine the best possible coverageyou're your corporation (* See Compliance Checklist)

7.)   Establish Program Timeline/Details and Referral Network

    a.)   **CRITIAL QUESTIONS:** What is your target population? What are the outcomes? How long will clients need to stay in your program until outcomes are achieved? Is it open to both men and women? What age group? What credentials do you and your staff posess? How much does it cost to refer a student to the program? What is your program budget?

    b.)   Prepare a short presentation to some of your key referral entities and make the request for a small cohort of student for a trial run (*see Connection Web for more details).

8.)   Establish a Volunteer Team

    a.)   *See Key Player Checklist for more details

9.)   Create The Consistent Community

    a.)   Do your clients know when and where to find you at ALL times? Start-up operation does not need to be constant (don't quit your day job… yet) but you do need to set a schedule and stick to it consistently so that you set up a precedent for accountability. You are always on time, you always keep your commitments.

10.)   Do Not Deviate

    a.)   Start up is a time for consistency, you can modify the ABC program and its practices after you have established your existence for 6 months. Keep your commitment to the plan that you provided your donors and the outcomes that you promised to your referral entities. The donors and the referral agencies are the keys to your existence and they MUST understand that you are focused during this start-up phase.

11.)   Report, Report, Report

    a.)   Constant connection to the referral entities. Have you updated them each week on the progress of their/your clients (every week should include an email update)? Have you tracked how their referrals are progressing toward intended outcomes? Have you asked for ways that you can improve your service offerings?

Chapter 3
Key Player Checklist

The following list identifies all of the individuals who will be instrumental to the start up of the ABC corporation. Not all of these individuals need to be financially compensated for their work at the corporation's outset, but their ideas and input need to be included in the start-up decision making processes. As funds become available, some of these individuals can be invited to continue as paid staff members. The list below identifies a sample hierarchy of positions in the ABC corporation (1-highest rank, 7-lowest rank).

1.) Board of Directors (governed by pre-established Bylaws)
    a.) Chairperson- needs to have non-profit management experience
    b.) Vice-Chairperson- needs to have non-profit management experience
    c.) Treasurer- needs to have financial services/accounting background
    d.) Secretary- needs to have clerical/note-taking experience
    e.) Other general board members- each board member needs to bring a diverse perspective to the organization. Each member must represent one area of the services that ABC corp. provides its clients. For example: if ABC corp. provides exercise classes, you need a certified fitness professional advising you on the Board of Directors
2.) Founder/Executive Director
    a.) Visionary, Fundraiser, Motivator
3.) Chief Operating Officer
    a.) Controls/manages the day-to-day operation of your facility and oversees the services for the clients. Leads, manages, and trains all of the staff.
4.) Chief Financial Officer
    a.) Works with the Treasurer and Executive Director to manage the financial resources of the corporation.
5.) Staff (eventually paid staff)
    a.) These are the members of your team who interact with the students most of all, and who drive the outcomes for the students.
6.) Staff (volunteer staff)
    a.) These are team members who come occasionally to provide specific coaching/presentations for students
7.) Contractors (paid)
    a.) Specifically research specialists who can support your efforts in quantifying the proposed outcomes of your program. How will you collect data and how will you analyze data? Having a contractor help you with this is the key to achieving sustainable results going forward.

A few additional notes concerning the Board of Directors and initial staff:

- In the interest of honesty, when most people choose their original board of directors, they just pick family members and friends who they know and trust. Most people are cautious with their new/young corporation, and so they don't want to bring on people who will try to mess up their "founder's vision." That's why it sometimes makes sense to go with people who you know and trust and are certain that they will give you the freedom to run things the way that you want to (at least at the start). Plus, when you pick this first group of board of directors you ONLY give them the ability to sit on the board for one year (most board terms are closer to three years). Because they are only one the board for one year, it takes the pressure off of the situation. If they are great, they stay! If they are not great, then you have a whole year to find a new board member to replace them. All of that specific language will be in your bylaws.
- You need board members to be local people who live in your area and CARE about your area. Your original board and your board (certainly after the first year) need to be BIG donors (if possible) so that they can help fund you and get you off of the ground. It is even a good idea to have some board members who are willing to come down and volunteer at your program as well. As time goes on, you need to select board members strategically based off of the things that your program needs. For example, If your program needs financial help, you will need to find a local financial consultant to sit on your board. Your board of directors can be small at first (perhaps 5 people) but eventually you can consider expanding up to as many members as your bylaws permit. Your board members also need to be outspoken people who will help you to promote the business and help you get the word out at the beginning.
- As for your team of people who actually work "on the ground with you," the hard truth is that you might need to do it alone for a while before anyone comes on board to join you. I had to run Bench Mark Program solo for almost an entire year before I got any help at all. Keep your number of students small at first, and just do a GREAT job working with them. Word will spread about what you are doing and the right people will come alongside you. You'll have to work hard, alone, and be patient though... that was a hard lesson for me to learn. But trust me, if you lead by example in your organization, the right people WILL become interested in what you are doing. No one is going to do the job of bringing life to your vision as well as you are, so just go solo for a while, do the best that you can, share your story, and people will find you. Impact the kids who you begin with and then motivate them to work with you to help others in need! That is the true key to sustainable growth: helping someone, and then helping them to help others. The more that you tell people about who you are, what you do, and why it works, the more people will come banging on your door asking to join you.

Chapter 4
Legal/Financial Compliance Checklist

As a start-up corporation, it will be nearly impossible for you to follow "the rules" perfectly. As ABC corp. grows, you will learn how to legally and financially "stay in line" because other professionals will be watching you and advising you. However, at the start, it is important to make sure that all of these needs have been met so that you and your staff are free and clear of unnecessary liability and risk.

You MUST have:
1.   Articles of Incorporation*, Bylaws*, Board of Directors, EIN number*, Board meeting minutes (for each meeting you conduct), Quarterly Financial Report (produced by your Chief Financial Officer and Board Treasurer), Annual Report (produced once each year by the Executive Director and Board Chairperson).
2.   Bank Account (NOT the founder's personal account)
3.   General Liability Insurance and Executive/Director's Insurance
4.   If working with youth, all staff need Child Abuse Clearances (plus other clearances mandated by your state)
5.   Policy and Procedure Manual (again you can write this on your own or find helpful samples online.
6.   IF staff are paid, you need a 3rd party* payroll executive to administer pay
7.   3rd party accountant to audit your program (or perform a less intensive "financial review") each year. See your Board Treasurer or qualified CPA for details.

* Many of the items listed in #1 will be acquired/written/created with the help of an attorney or other legal counsel. Of course, you can find resources online to script these documents on your own, but seeking professional legal counsel will streamline this process and help you avoid costly errors in the future.
*3rd party refers to someone who is unaffiliated with your organization (no conflict of interest)

Chapter 5
Connection Web | Generating Referrals

Referrals will be the fuel for your program, because with each referral comes the potential for financial support. You'll need to network with these key players in your local community to present the program and offer up your services:

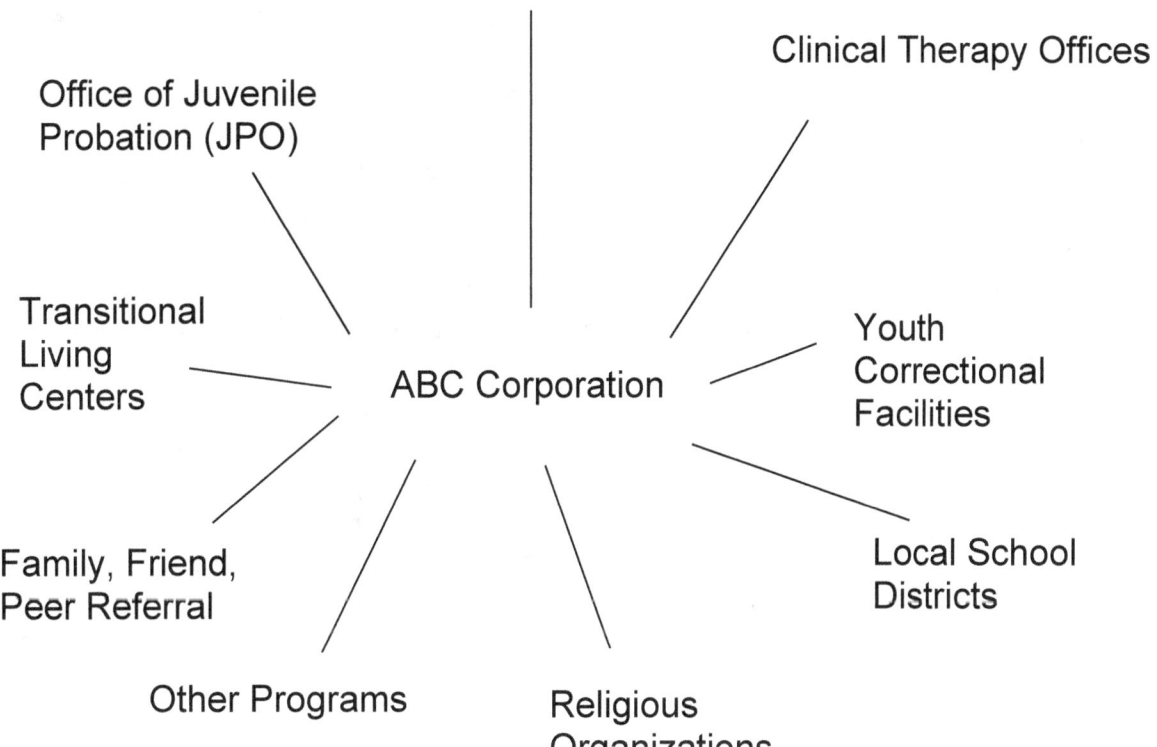

How exactly will you network and connect with each of these entities? You'll soon learn that they are all interconnected, and that at-risk youth flow through each of these organizations. Your first step should be to make one connection within one of these entities, establish trust for your program, and then ask for a connection to the next agency on your list. Because probation officers are well connected and generally seeking positive programming for their clients, it may be wise to begin networking within that office in order to establish ABC corporation. If your services go above and beyond what these agencies think you can provide for your clients, word will spread about your program. Conversely, if your services are sub-standard, word will also spread quickly that your program is not worth the while.

Chapter 6
Conversation Break-down Sheet | School District and Guidance Counselors

The school district(s) where your clients are enrolled has a vested interest in each student but often lack the personnel to provide each at-risk youth with the smaller group mentoring that they need. Therefore school districts reach out to community partners to establish after-school mentoring services. Your initial contacts with the school district might be: school resource officers, guidance counselors, vice principals, student service coordinators, program coordinators of the ENTIRE district, extended-day coordinators for the ENTIRE district.

A conversation breakdown with these individuals is as follows:

School District Official (SDO): Tell me about your program and what you have to offer to our students?

You: ABC Corporation is looking to partner with the school district in order to enhance some of the mentoring services that are already present in the district's programming. We have a model for small group mentoring that we believe could improve the lives of at-risk youth living in the district. *At this point, see "Model Description" in Chapter 13 for a sample, in-depth description of your model.

SDO: How do you plan to enhance the mentoring services that we already provide? We actually already partner with other organization's similar to ABC Corp.

You: The reason why I called this meeting is because I believe that my organization's approach is unique from the approach being taken by the other mentoring programs. At ABC corporation we tailor our mentorship to students who need a physical outlet for their stress, anxiety, anger, and other charged emotions. Our program targets youth who haven't felt comfortable in other programming, or who have given up on other programming. By offering a very hands-off, unassuming environment, we encourage students to first "be themselves" before we ask them who they "want to become." Our mentoring and coaching practices are then tailored to that student's needs and their unique life circumstances. *Your challenge here is to point out the unique differentiators in your program WITHOUT purposefully degrading the work of other similar programs operating in your area.

SDO: How can we verify that your services are as impactful as you propose? What evidence do you have?

You: ABC Corporation was created to model other highly successful programs across the country (reference: Innercity Weightlifting, Bench Mark Program, Crushers Club, Beat The Streets etc.). We recently completed a 3-month pilot program with a small group of at-risk youth and all of them achieved these outcomes: (here is where you talk about the success of your trial-run). We would like to offer a similar pilot program with a group of students from your district, selected by your staff and guidance counselors who know the student's best. If given 3-months, we can improve the lives of those few students by introducing them into ABC Corp's mentoring environment. We can then evaluate the program together after those 3-months to determine if we can expand our partnership in the future.

SDO: How much will it cost our district to launch this pilot program with you?

You: ABC Corp will offer you the 3-month pilot program free of charge. Our board of directors and a committed group of private donors have helped fund each pilot period of program because they believe in the power of our program to produce results in that short amount of time. This is a low-risk opportunity for your district, but with high-value yields in the lives of these students. Any partnership that we establish beyond the 3-month trial period will be supported by a per-diem program fee that we will budget for based on the number of students that attend our program from your office.

Chapter 7
Conversation Break-down Sheet | Juvenile Probation

The Office of Juvenile Probation has direct access to the population that ABC Corp intends to serve, and therefore this office is a wonderful place to introduce your program. The Office of Juvenile Probation also has access to the funding that can sustain your program, if you can provide enough value to its Officers. You can provide value to the probation officers by helping to "lighten their caseload," and helping at-risk teens to complete their probation requirements.

Your initial contact at this office should be the Director.

Juvenile Probation Officer (JPO): Tell me about your program and what you have to offer to juvenile delinquents in our area?

You: ABC Corporation is a program that I developed in order to support your office and improve the outcomes of young people who find themselves on juvenile probation. Our program offers an extracurricular support to at-risk youth who are defiant and are struggling to complete their probation requirements. We use exercise to surround them with a group of positive mentors, and through casual conversation, help them to realize their potential to succeed. Our mentors are successful adults who grew up under the same circumstances as these youth. Our program will only work if we can work together to serve youth who are struggling, and so collaboration between your officers and our staff is paramount to our student's success.

JPO: How long have you been doing this work, and what other community partners are involved:

You: Our organization is a relatively new one but we have created a model based off of programming used by other successful businesses such as (reference: InnerCity Weightlifting, Bench Mark Program, etc.). We know that mentoring is an evidence based practice, and thanks to a short pilot program that we just completed, we believe that we have proof of concept (here you can talk about how your pilot program went, and how many kids you were able to help). We are forging partnerships with the local school district, local clinical therapy offices, as well as the children and youth agency in order to provide direct access into our gym facilities. The most important connection however, is with your office in particular. We believe that your officers could be our most valuable community partners when helping to provide opportunities for the at-risk youth who we serve who might benefit from our unique environment.

JPO: How exactly does this all "work" though? Can you explain the program a bit?

You: ABC Corp creates a comfortable space for students to express themselves, be themselves, and let go of their anxieties. Through a busy gym facility, youth can use their bodies, improve their self confidence, and surprise themselves with their strength, all while being coached by professional trainers. We use exercise to create a space for conversation between mentor and student, which is the tool that we use to enact change. Students regularly return to our space because they know there they can find an adult mentor to confide in, to ask the tough questions, and to exercise off any unhealthy emotions. When our mentors become aware of the needs of each student, we gather to discuss ways that we can support each student. In addition to what we call "general life coaching" between mentor and student, as a team we are prepared to offer academic tutoring for students who need help in school and career workshops for students who need to make some money through a job (resume writing, interview skills, etc.). The program runs each and every night, giving kids a consistent place to find positivity and work toward career and academic goals set by their mentors, probation officers, guidance counselors, and others.

JPO: How do we get started, and how much will this cost us?

You: I would like to make a presentation to your probation officers at the next full staff meeting in order to explain my program to everyone. Then I would propose that we start with a trial run of 10 students from a handful of your probation officer's. I will report back to each officer who refers a student on a weekly basis, and after 3 months if the outcomes are acceptable, we will discuss the costs associated with continuing to utilize our program's services. At this time, our board of directors and donors have committed to help fund this trial run phase because they believe in the results that our program can produce. I will be happy to sit down with you in a follow-up meeting to outline our budget and discuss per-diem fees associated with our program.

Chapter 8
Conversation Break-Down Sheet | Clinical Therapy Offices

Clinical Therapy Offices will serve as a wonderful support to your program. Your relationship with their offices may or may not result in financial support for your program, but the connection to for-profit clinical therapy offices can "pay-off" in other ways. For example, our connection to them will lend credibility to your organization. Working with clinical therapists demonstrates to others that you are trying to serve the "whole individual," meaning while they are in therapy and out of therapy as well.

Clinical Therapist (CT): I've heard about your program through a few of my clients as well as a few probation officers. I'm intrigued to learn what exactly your program does?

You: ABC Corp is a new local business that brings consistent and supportive mentors into the lives of at-risk youth in order to generate long term positive outcomes after therapy and probation. Our goal is to fit into the lives of at-risk teenagers around other supportive structures such as yourself (the therapist), probation officers, school guidance counselors, etc. If you have heard about us through other service providers, then we must be effectively communicating! Our hope is that we can give at-risk youth a fun and supportive environment to build their confidence and self esteem while they are receiving other services from therapist and probation officers, then once those services end, ABC corp services will continue. Together we can invest in a supportive structure for students that goes far beyond our immediate future and can become a stable foundation for them to build on the framework for success that we are creating today.

CT: If I send a youth to your program, what exactly will happen to them?

You: Youth who are referred to our program will be contacted by myself personally as Executive Director, or by another program official helping me with student in-take. We will chat with the student and parental guardian and offer to meet at our facility or to come to the home and meet, if the student prefers. The goal of our initial meeting is to learn about the youth, their challenges, and their goals. From the first meeting we can learn what mentors might best connect with the youth at our facility, and when the youth does come to the facility, we will have someone ready to show them around. From that point forward it is up to the youth to determine how they want to engage with the program. They may choose to dive into exercise, dive into conversation with mentors, sit back and enjoy the music, or work on the computer. Regardless of how they engage with the program, youth will constantly be invited to join mentors in various activities around the gym. While attendance is voluntary, youth who enjoy the space/environment tend to return just to soak up some of the positive energy in our facility. As time goes on and relationship of trust and respect form between mentor and youth, we as a team are able to support youth in more than just physical endeavors, but also academic and career endeavors as well.

CT: So what is the catch? How is this program funded and how much will it cost us?

You: We are happy to offer up our services to your office for free. We would only ask that if you believe our services are beneficial, to please complete a formal letter of support for us to list to our supporters. Currently our organization is funded by a group of private donors as well as our board of directors. We are moving toward contract funding from the Office of Juvenile Probation, the School District, and the Children and Youth Agency. At this time, we would like to "pilot" our relationship without asking for funding. If we see value and positive results in the lives of youth between our programs, then perhaps we can discuss funding at a later date. Currently, we would like to invite you and your staff to refer up to 10 young men and women to a 3-month trial program at our organization.

*CLARIFICATION: Why would we ask government funded agencies to fund our program and not privately run clinical therapy offices? The principal behind this practice is this: when you provide services to a government funded agency for free, they enjoy the services and get used to the services provided as "free." When you provide a private-sector business with free services, you build credibility and rapport, and if you are not careful, they TOO will get used to your services as "free." However, when you provide free services to the private sector you are building a bit of leverage, and that leverage is useful once or twice a year when you have your big fundraising campaign. At those times, you reach back out to the executives at the privately owned clinical therapy offices and you remind them of your good work while asking for a donation. These individuals, if your work is legitimately effective (and if they like you), can give you access to a donor base that is unlike any other (generally very wealthy). If you help these business executives, they will help you! Because they are in the private sector and (if they are doing well) have a budget surplus, they will very often reward you with a donation for your good work while also spreading news about your program to other donors as well. If the operation of your business relieves or improves the operation of their business, you're on the right track.

Chapter 9
Conversation Break-Down Sheet | Other Programs and Detention Centers

No matter where you are, other programs will be present that offer similar services to a similar target demographic. As a rule of thumb, their business does not concern you nor does their success or failure as a program concern you unless it has a direct impact (positive or negative) on the students that you serve. If you become aware of a partnership opportunity that is mutually beneficial to both organizations and most importantly the common clientele that you serve, you should call a meeting of your advisors and proceed with caution. Partnerships are never as simple as they seem, and any partnership decisions need to be reviewed by attorney's, financial advisors, and boards of directors as a whole before official agreements are signed. Remember, there are plenty of at-risk youth in your area, and no single program will be able to satisfy them all. The following is a dialogue modeling conversation with a local detention center, which is generally a partner worth networking with.

Youth Detention Center (YDC): Tell me about your program and why you are contacting our center about you operation?

You: ABC Corp has been operating a pilot program with the local office of juvenile probation and the children and youth agency. We know that many of the youth that we are serving through the office of juvenile probation pass through your facility before they enter ours. I wanted to reach out to you to brainstorm ways that our organization might be able to become involved with these youth while they are still under your care in your facility? I would like to come into your facility and offer exercise programming to youth in the hope of directing them to my program after they are released from your facility. In this way, I could provide a service to you by operating exercise classes once per week in your facility, and you could provide a service to me by allowing me to network with at-risk while they are detained.

YDC: I can put you in touch with our volunteer coordinator to find a time for you to come in and work with our students, but how much will this cost us?

You: I would be more than happy to operate my exercise program in your facility for four free sessions. If your staff and residents enjoy the services, we can discuss an appropriate payment for me to continue with these services. I will only ask that you pay for the value of my time as if I was working with a personal training client, because I am a certified personal trainer. My hourly rate is _____.

YDC: Are you prepared to work with unruly kids who don't pay any attention to you or follow your rules?

You: I am prepared to work with the youth in your facility because I understand their and their circumstances better than they imagine. My goal is to help youth see a path directly out of the detention center and into a successful future. If I can network with them in your facility, even if they don't pay much attention to me, then they are more likely to attend my program when they are released from your facility. If they see me on the streets, they are more likely to recognize me when I approach them and ask them how they are doing. If they get used to seeing me and get to know me, then I can begin to serve as a consistent structure in their lives, something that they can lean on and depend on.

Chapter 10
Conversation Break-Down Sheet | Donors

The first conversation with donors might seem daunting, but if you have a fear of "the ask," just remember that you are not asking for funding for yourself, you are asking for funding for those people who do not have the voice to ask for themselves. Remind yourself before every meeting with a prospective donor that you have the privilege to speak on behalf of all of the unheard voices in your city, and when you ask a donor to support your vision, you are giving that donor the opportunity to impact those hundreds (maybe even thousands) of unheard voices through you. If someone chooses to support you with their donor dollars, then you must commit to them that you will put their dollars to work to lift up the down-trodden, and blaze a path where others can follow in your footsteps. If you worry that the donor will not recognize the impact that you have, make a promise that you will provide concrete results, and stick to that promise.

Here are a few tips when going into a meeting with a prospective donor:

1.) Every donor wants to feel special, so open with a conversation focused on THEM. Learn about their interests, their history of support, WHY they are charitable, and how they came to learn about you? Do not make the donor feel like you singled them out because of their net worth. Whether you did single them out for that reason or not, donors "give" because you make them feel involved, so your main focus needs to be helping them understand how they can expand their personal philanthropy and become a part of your organizational family.

2.) Be open about your organization's current financial position. There is no shame in starting small, and if you lie about your size and success of your program, you have everything to lose. You need to stand out as a refreshing young leader who does not attempt to mask hidden limitations in order to gain a few extra dollars. The non-profit world, and the business community as a whole, is riddled with exaggeration, and you want to make sure that you are clear and transparent with your financial position.

3.) Bring along hand-outs! Your donors always need a take-away. Material should be one-page, and to-the-point. An essential handout to be included is a copy of your program's budget. Prospective donors need to see where/how you spend your money, and how much of your money is spent on "overhead" vs. "client services." Use the handouts to exemplify some of your success stories, or students who have been able to positively transform their lives thanks to you.

4.) Remember, early donors are supporting YOU and not the program (not yet). They will give their dollars to your organization because they believe in YOUR capacity to handle their money appropriately and to create something that goes beyond your time. Do not give them any reason to believe that you might not be the perfect recipient of their donor dollars. Express your gratitude with a hand-written note immediately after the meeting. These little thank you notes (even if there was no donation) set you above and beyond the rest.

5.) There is no formula to winning the biggest dollar amount from any given donor. However, if you treat donors with the same level of respect you would treat a friend or family member, they will feel welcomed by you and more likely to donate to you. Donors are REGULAR PEOPLE, and if you invest your time in learning about THEM, they will likely invest their philanthropic resources in YOU. Donations (many times from the same individual) grow over time with effective stewardship of the donor. Stick with the Golden Rule when stewarding a donor: "Treat others as you would want to be treated."

Chapter 11

Staffing/Volunteer Guidelines:

Your staff and your volunteers MUST feel as though you respect them and support them. Working with at-risk youth can raise tension between staff members, and a consistent rulebook or set of guidelines for your staff will help to mitigate any disputes that arise. The example below is a simplified sample of a guideline sheet and additional, certainly more in-depth, policy/procedure resources can be found at the National Mentoring Partnership website. See below for sample staff guidelines created by Bench Mark Program staff:

Mentor Guidelines

1. **Applications for PA Child Abuse Clearance, FBI Background Check, and PA Criminal History Report should be made within 2-weeks of initial involvement. Copies of these clearances should be placed on file with BMP as soon as they arrive.**

2. **No mentors under 21 years of age.**

3. **All new mentors participate in orientation with BMP staff.** New mentors will also shadow staff for one gym session to acclimate to the environment. Until clearances are on file with BMP, mentors should not be alone with students.

4. **Mentors should maintain consistent attendance of at least 2 hours each week.** Our students depend on your consistency, as you will likely become one of the only consistent influences in their lives. Connecting with BMP students takes time and commitment. Students notice the investment of your time. Because of this, we ask that you commit to spending at least one hour each time you come to the gym.

5. **Mentors should demonstrate the ability to listen more, talk less.** BMP students need to feel comfortable opening up to you about their circumstances without the fear that you will immediately tell them what to do. Mentoring is a two-way street: listen to the student, show them respect, ask questions, and discuss solutions together.

6. **Mentors should examine their own prejudices or stereotypes prior to entering the gym facility and be open to discussion about these topics with other mentors.** Prejudices are something that we all carry in one form or another. Unconscious prejudice can sometimes make it difficult to work with other people in an unbiased manner. Some of our students have had experiences that make them particularly reactive or sensitive to other prejudice. Because of this, we ask that you be open to learning new things and to checking your own reactions when difficult situations arise.

7. **Mentors should always ask for permission before having contact with BMP students outside of the gym facility. Mentors should also provide a summary of planned activities to the Executive Director.** Under various circumstances, the BMP Executive Director will grant permission to support a student outside of the gym facility. After 1-2 weeks of consistent participation and attendance at the gym, mentors may begin to establish contact with students and families outside the gym as needed to a accomplish student goals. (Ex. transport to job interview).

8.   Mentors should offer advice based on their own personal experience and expertise. This may include advice about physical fitness, academics, family/peer relationships, and/or career advancement, among many other things. You do NOT have to exercise with students to perform as a mentor. Stories of your own personal struggles and experiences offer meaningful ways to connect with the youth at our program. If you are unsure what advice to give in a situation, please pull another mentor into the discussion. There are many ways to consistently support our students through involvement in the BMP Family.

END- Sample Guidelines

Before involvement in the program, all prospective staff members are asked to sign these guidelines (and initial beside each bullet point) to verify that they are in agreement with the facility protocols. It is also advised that you and your staff discuss establishing a protocol for when it is appropriate to ask a student to leave your facility. Under what circumstances can you remove a student from the program? How many adults are needed to make a decision of that magnitude? What is the minimum age limit of students in your facility.

Although you may be tempted to open your doors to EVERYONE in the neighborhood, if you do not protect the space for your target age group, you will effectively scare your target age group away. PLEASE take the time to establish your basic rules (such as age limit) before the opening night of your program and post the rules in multiple places around your facility for all to see. Enforcing the rules will be much easier if you have them posted around your facility.

If you and your team decide that it would be helpful, you might also consider establishing a set of student guidelines as well. You can have incoming students read the guidelines and sign them in agreement with the guidelines. Students and staff alike will benefit from the structure and commitment that you establish in your facility.

Chapter 12
Grant Writing Checklist

During your start-up phase, you will likely hear friends, family, and a slew of random people suggest that you pursue funding through grants. Unfortunately, grant writing is something that most people assume is easily accessible for all organizations, when really that is not the case. Here are some items that you need in order to work with most granting agencies/foundations. * of course there are certainly exceptions to these requirements

1.	2-3 years of audited program financial statements
2.	501 (c) 3 status
3.	Inclusion into your state's bureau of charitable organizations
4.	2-3 years of data to support the claim that your program is successful
5.	Well written letter of intent
6.	Well written organizational budget
7.	Well written program budget (specific to the grant)
8.	Well written executive summary
9.	Multiple letters of support from community partners
10.	Invitation from the granting agency to submit your application

If you do not have these items lined up at the outset of your grant application, you might want to consider pursuing other funding opportunities simply because the time and effort required to compile all of this material might not be worth the potential for rejection. Some agencies choose not to apply for grants unless they get a written invitation from an individual from the foundation first!

Here are a few other funding sources (sometimes more lucrative) for start-up corporations.

1.	Private Donors: friends, family, community members (church members)
2.	Corporate Donors: Local businesses
3.	Community Foundations: often will offer start-up funding.

QUESTION: How will you obtain the start-up funding that you need for your trial run?

You'll need "quick money" with no strings attached, therefore allowing you to spend it as you please. This money is likely to be raised from private donors. And what if your family and friends are not capable of pitching in to inject the start-up capital that you need? You'll have to begin working your way through your networks, asking everyone you know if they know someone who has the capacity to help found your organization and the crucial trial run period. Closer than you think, there are individuals with the capacity to help get your trial run off of the ground. When all else fails, you can leverage church groups to access kind hearted, often-deep-pocketed, individuals. You might even get lucky and run into an individual who donates spaCce instead of money! At this point in your growth you need to hustle hard to bring in the start-up dollars. If your trial run is successful, and you use your proof of concept to produce positive results in the lives of kids that you serve, then the next round of funding will be easy to raise.

Just remember, be CLEAR with potential donors about how much you need, WHY you need that much, and exactly HOW you intend to spend it.

Chapter 13
Model Description

When you begin to present your organization to potential donors or other local organizations, you may have to field the question: "What model is your program based on?" or some iteration of that question. The simple answer is this: "My program does not operate out of any existing model. I formed it with components of successful programs across the country, but the model, or "system" that I have created is my own."

Of course, you will then have to describe how the system you created actually works! Here is a sample for how students flow through Bench Mark Program and how we visually represent the model.

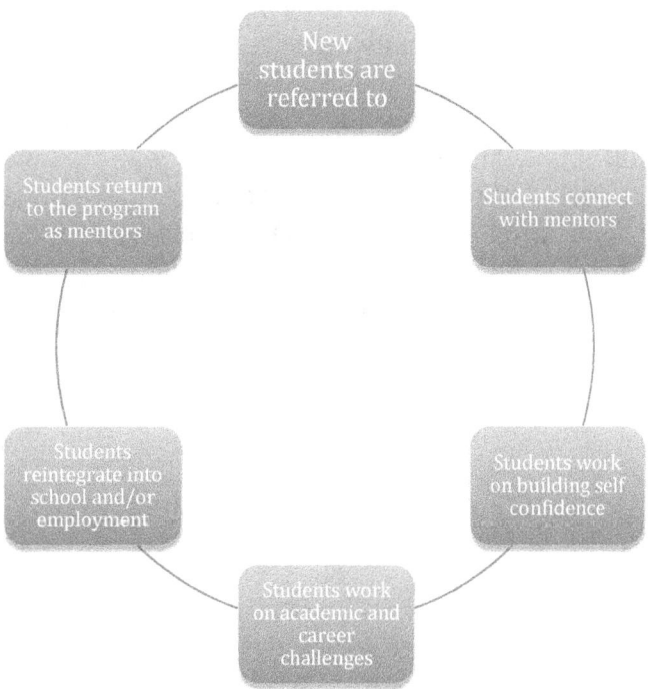

The way that you visually represent your model will be different from what is displayed above, but when people ask you about the model or "structure" of your organization, this is what you will walk them through:

1. Explain the referral process and how youth enter your program

2. Explain what happens to students once they become involved in the program

3. Explain the goals you have for each student, how you work toward those goals, and give a timeline

4. Explain how students graduate from your program, what is the end goal?

5.   Explain how students can feed back into the program, and "pay it forward"

If you are in a conversation with an individual who wants to better understand your "model" or "structure" then this is the path that you need to walk them through.

You might also consider using these words/phrases to describe your work:

1.   A comfortable place for youth to come and express themselves, only asking for help when they feel ready.

2.   An unassuming environment where we let youth direct their own support plan and strategy

3.   A place that feels natural to youth, in other words, a space where they would come and hang out even if they did not have any negativity in their lives. Our environment doesn't feel like a "treatment facility"

4.   We provide a viable alternative to life on the streets. In other words, our model gives youth the family they are craving, the respect they deserve, and the opportunity for advancement that they need to feel excited about their lives

5.   Our program provides consistent care and support over the long-term, creating a model for other programs that want to invest in the lives of youth over a longer period of time in order to generate more impactful outcomes.

6.   Our program is set up to use exercise as a tool to generate conversation and build self-confidence. What follows is a relationship between mentor/student that allows our team to get to the heart of the issues that are holding youth down in life. Our model uses exercise as the "hook" and academics and career support as the change-makers once a relationship of trust has been established.

www.ingramcontent.com/pod-product-compliance
Lightning Source LLC
Chambersburg PA
CBHW081756170526
45167CB00009B/4043